The Remedy of Love

The Remedy of Love

Ovid

MINT EDITIONS

Remedia Amoris; or, The Remedy of Love was written in 2AD.

This edition published by Mint Editions 2020.

ISBN 9781513280257 | E-ISBN 9781513285276

Published by Mint Editions®

MINT EDITIONS

minteditionbooks.com

Publishing Director: Jennifer Newens
Design & Production: Rachel Lopez Metzger
Project Manager: Micaela Clark
Translated by Henry T. Riley
Typesetting: Westchester Publishing Services

The God of Love had read the title and the name of this treatise, when he said, "War, I see, war is being meditated against me." Forbear, Cupid, to accuse thy Poet of such a crime; me, who so oft have borne thy standards with thee for my leader. I am no son of Tydeus, wounded by whom, thy mother returned into the yielding air with the steeds of Mars. Other youths full oft grow cool; I have ever loved; and shouldst thou inquire what I am doing even now, I am still in love. Besides, I have taught by what arts thou mayst be won; and that which is now a system, was an impulse before. Neither thee do I betray, sweet Boy, nor yet my own arts; nor has my more recent Muse unravelled her former work.

If any one loves an object which he delights to love, enraptured, in his happiness, let him rejoice, and let him sail with prospering gales. But if any one impatiently endures the sway of some cruel fair, that he may not be undone, let him experience relief from my skill. Why has one person, tying up his neck by the tightened halter, hung, a sad burden, from the lofty beam? Why, with the hard iron, has another pierced his own entrails? Lover of peace, thou dost bear the blame of their deaths. He, who, unless he desists, is about to perish by a wretched passion, let him desist; and then thou wilt prove the cause of death to none. Besides, thou art a boy; and it becomes thee not to do aught but play. Play on; a sportive sway befits thy years. Far thou mayst use thy arrows, when drawn from the quiver for warfare; but thy weapons are free from deadly blood.

Let thy stepfather Mars wage war both with the sword and the sharp lance; and let him go, as victor, blood-stained with plenteous slaughter. Do thou cherish thy mother's arts, which, in safety, we pursue; and by the fault of which no parent he comes bereft. Do thou cause the portals to be burst open in the broils of the night; and let many a chaplet cover the decorated doors. Cause the youths and the bashful damsels to meet in secret; and by any contrivance they can, let them deceive their watchful husbands. And at one moment, let the lover utter blandishments, at another, rebukes, against the obdurate door-posts; and, shut out, let him sing some doleful ditty. Contented with these tears, thou wilt be without the imputation of any death. Thy torch is not deserving to be applied to the consuming pile.

These words said I. Beauteous Love waved his resplendent wings, and said to me, "Complete the work that thou dost design." Come, then, ye deceived youths, for my precepts; ye whom your passion has deceived in every way. By him, through whom you have learned how to love, learn how to be cured; for you, the same hand shall cause the wound and the remedy. The earth nourishes wholesome plants, and the same produces injurious ones; and full oft is the nettle the neighbour of the rose. That lance which once made a wound in the enemy, the son of Hercules, afforded a remedy for that wound. But whatever is addressed to the men, believe, ye fair, to be said to you as well; to both sides am I giving arms. If of these any are not suited to your use, still by their example they may afford much instruction. My useful purpose is to extinguish the raging flames, and not to have the mind the slave of its own imperfections. Phyllis would have survived, if she had employed me as her teacher; and along that road, by which nine times she went, she would have gone oftener still. And Dido, dying, would not have beheld from the summit of her tower the Dardanian ships giving their sails to the wind.

Grief, too, would not have armed Medea, the mother against her own offspring; she who took vengeance on her husband, by the shedding of their united blood. Through my skill, Tereus, although Philomela did captivate him, would not, through his crimes, have been deserving to become a bird.

Give me Pasiphaë for a pupil, at once she shall lay aside her passion for the bull; give me Phædra, the shocking passion of Phædra shall depart. Bring Paris back to us; Menelaus shall possess his Helen, and Pergamus shall not fall, conquered by Grecian hands. If impious Scylla had read my treatise, the purple lock, Nisus, would have remained upon thy head. With me for your guide, ye men, repress your pernicious anxieties; and onward let the bark proceed with the companions, me the pilot. At the time when you were learning how to love, Naso was to be studied; now, too, will the same Naso have to be studied by you. An universal assertor of liberty, I will relieve the breasts that are oppressed by their tyrants; do you show favour, each of you, to my liberating wand.

Prophetic Phoebus, inventor of song, and of the healing art, I pray that the laurel may afford me its aid. Do thou shew favour both to the poet and to the physician; to thy guardianship is either care consigned.

While still you may, and while moderate emotions influence your breast; if you repent, withhold your footsteps upon the very threshold. Tread under foot the hurtful seeds of the sudden malady, while they are still fresh; and let your steed, as he begins to go, refuse to proceed. For time supplies strength, time thoroughly ripens the young grapes; and it makes that into vigorous standing corn, which before was only blades of grass. The tree which affords its extending shade to those who walk beneath, was but a twig at the time when it was first planted. At that time, with the hand it could have been rooted from the surface of the earth; now, increased by its own powers, it is standing upon a large space. Examine with active perception, what sort of object it is, with which you are in love; and withdraw your neck from a yoke that is sure to gall. Resist the first advances; too late is a cure attempted, when through long hesitation the malady has waxed strong. But hasten, and do not postpone to a future moment; that which is not agreeable to-day, will to-morrow be still less so. Every passion is deceiving, and finds nutriment in delay. Each day's morrow is the best suited for liberty.

You see but few rivers arise from great sources; most of them are multiplied by a collection of waters. If thou hadst at once perceived how great a sin thou wast meditating, thou wouldst not, Myrrha, have had thy features covered with bark. I have seen a wound, which at first was curable, when neglected receive injury from protracted delay. But because we are delighted to pluck the flowers of Venus, we are continually saying, "This will be done to-morrow just as well." In the meantime, the silent flames are gliding into the entrails; and the hurtful tree is sending its roots more deep.

But if the time for early aid has now passed by, and an old passion is seated deeply in your captured breast, a greater labour is provided; but, because I am called in but late to the sick, he shall not be deserted by me. With unerring hand the hero, son of Peeas, ought at once to have cutout the part in which he was wounded. Still, after many a year, he is supposed, when cured, to have given a finishing hand to the warfare. I, who just now was hastening to dispel maladies at their birth, am now tardy in administering aid to you at a later moment. Either try, if you can, to extinguish the flames when recent; or when they have become exhausted by their own efforts. When frenzy is in full career, yield to frenzy in its career; each impulse presents a difficult access. The swimmer is a fool, who, when he can cross the stream by going down with it sideways, struggles to go straight against the tide. A mind impatient, and not yet manageable by any contrivance, rejects the words of an adviser, and holds them in contempt. More successfully, then, shall I attempt it when he shall now allow his wounds to be touched, and shall be accessible to the words of truthfulness.

Who, but one bereft of understanding, would forbid a mother to weep at the death of her son? On such an occasion she is not to be counselled. When she shall have exhausted her tears, and have satisfied her afflicted feelings; that grief of hers will be capable of being soothed with words. The healing art is generally a work of opportunity; wine, administered at the proper time, is beneficial, and administered at an unsuitable time, is injurious. And, besides, you may inflame maladies and irritate them by checking them; if you do not combat them at the fitting moment.' Therefore, when you shall seem to be curable by my skill, take care, and by my precepts shun the first approaches of idleness. 'Tis that which makes you love, 'tis that which supports it, when once it has caused it: that is the cause and the nutriment of the delightful malady.

If you remove all idleness, the bow of Cupid is broken, and his torch lies despised and without its light. As much as the plane-tree delights in wine, the multitude in the stream, and as much as the reed of the marsh in a slimy soil, so much does Venus love idleness. You who seek a termination of your passion, attend to your business; love gives way before business; then you will be safe. Inactivity, and immoderate slumbers under no control, gaming too, and the temples aching through much wine, take away all strength 'from the mind that is free from a wound. Love glides insidiously upon the unwary. That Boy is wont to attend upon slothfulness; he hates the busy. Give to the mind that is unemployed some task with which it may be occupied. There are the Courts, there are the laws, there are your friends for you to defend. Go into the ranks white with the civic gown; or else do you take up with the youthful duties of bloodstained Mars; soon will voluptuousness turn its back on you.

Lo! the flying Parthian, a recent cause for a great triumph, is now beholding the arms of Caesar on his own plains. Conquer equally the arrows of Cupid and of the Parthians, and bring back a two-fold trophy to the Gods of your country. After Venus had once been wounded by the Ætolian spear, she entrusted wars to be waged by her lover.

Do you enquire why Ægisthus became an adulterer? The cause is self-evident; he was an idler. Others were fighting at Ilium, with slowly prospering arms: the whole of Greece had transported thither her strength. If he would have given his attention to war, she was nowhere waging it; or if to the Courts of law, Argos was free from litigation. What he could, he did; that he might not be doing nothing, he fell in love. Thus does that Boy make his approaches, so does that Boy take up his abode.

The country, too, soothes the feelings, and the pursuits of agriculture: any anxiety whatever may give way before this employment. Bid the tamed oxen place their necks beneath their burden, that the crooked ploughshare may wound the hard ground. Cover the grain of Ceres with the earth turned up, which the field may restore to you with bounteous interest. Behold the branches bending beneath the weight of the apples; how its own tree can hardly support the weight which it has produced. See the rivulets trickling along with their pleasing murmur; see the sheep, as they crop the fertile mead. Behold how the she-goats climb the rocks, and the steep crags; soon will they be bringing back their distended udders for their kids. The shepherd is tuning his song on the unequal reeds; the dogs, too, a watchful throng, are not far off. In another direction the lofty woods are resounding with lowings; and the dam is complaining that her calf is missing. Why name the time when the swarms fly from the yew trees, placed beneath them, that the honey-combs removed may relieve the bending osiers of their weight? Autumn affords its fruit; summer is beauteous with its harvests; spring produces flowers; winter is made cheerful by the fire. At stated periods the rustic pulls the ripened grape, and beneath his naked foot the juice flows out; at stated periods he binds up the dried hay, and clears the mowed ground with the wide toothed rake.

You yourself may set the plant in the watered garden; you yourself may form the channels for the trickling stream. The grafting is now come; make branch adopt branch, and let one tree stand covered with the foliage of another. When once these delights have begun to soothe your mind, Love, robbed of his power, departs with flagging wings.

Or do you follow the pursuit of hunting. Full oft has Venus, overcome by the sister of Phoebus, retreated in disgrace. Now follow the fleet hare with the quick-scented hound; now stretch your toils on the shady mountain ridge. Or else, alarm the timid deer with the variegated feather-foils; or let the boar fall, transfixed by the hostile spear. Fatigued, at night sleep takes possession of you, not thoughts of the fair; and with profound rest it refreshes the limbs. 'Tis a more tranquil pursuit, still it is a pursuit, on catching the bird, to win the humble prize, either with the net or with the bird-limed twigs; or else, to hide the crooked hooks of brass in morsels at the end, which the greedy fish may, to its destruction, swallow with its ravenous jaws.

Either by these, or by other pursuits, must you by stealth be beguiled by yourself, until you shall have learnt how to cease to love.

Only do you go, although you shall be detained by strong ties, go far away, and commence your progress upon a distant journey. You will weep when the name of your forsaken mistress shall recur to you: and many a time will your foot linger in the middle of your path. But the less willing you shall be to go, remember the more surely to go; persist; and compel your feet to hasten, however unwillingly. And don't you fear showers; nor let the Sabbaths of the stranger detain you; nor yet the Allia, so well known for its disasters. And don't enquire how many miles you have travelled, but how many are yet remaining for you; and invent no excuses, that you may remain near at hand. Neither do you count the hours, nor oft look back on Rome: but fly; still is the Parthian secure in flight from his foe.

Some one may style my precepts harsh: I confess that they are harsh; but that you may recover, you will have to endure much that is to be lamented. Full oft, when ill, I have drunk of bitter potions, though reluctantly; and when I entreated for it, food has been refused me. To cure your body, you will have to endure iron and fire; and though thirsty, you will not refresh your parched lips with water. That you may be healed in spirit, will you refuse to submit to anything? Inasmuch as that part is ever of greater value than the body. But still, most difficult is the access to my art; and the one labour is how to endure the first moments of separation. Do you perceive how the yoke, at first, galls the oxen when caught? how the new girth hurts the flying steed?

Perhaps you will be loth to depart from your paternal home. But still you will depart; then you will be longing to return. No paternal home, but the love of your mistress, cloaking its own faultiness by specious words, will be calling you back. When once you have gone, the country, and your companions, and the long journey will afford a thousand solaces for your sorrow. And do not think it is enough to depart; be absent for a long time, until the flame has lost its power and the ashes are without their fire. If you shall hasten to return, except with your judgment strengthened, rebellious Love will be wielding his cruel arms against you. Suppose that, although you shall have absented yourself, you return both hungry and thirsty; will not all this delay even act to your detriment?

If any one supposes that the noxious herbs of the Hæmonian lands and magic arts can be of avail, let him see to it. That is the old-fashioned method of sorcery; my Apollo, in his hallowed lines, is pointing out an innoxious art. Under my guidance, no ghost shall be summoned to come forth from the tomb; no hag with her disgusting spells shall cleave the ground. No crops of corn shall remove from one field into another; nor shall the disk of Phoebus suddenly be pale. Tiberinus shall flow into the waves of the ocean just as he is wont; just as she is wont, shall the Moon be borne by her snow-White steeds. No breasts shall lay aside their cares dispelled by enchantments; vanquished by virgin sulphur, love shall not take to flight.

Colchian damsel, what did the herbs of the Phasian land avail thee, when thou didst desire to remain in thy native home? Of what use, Circe, were the herbs of thy mother Persia to thee, when the favouring breeze bore away the barks of Neritos? Every thing didst thou do that thy crafty guest might not depart; still did he give his filled sails to an assured flight. Every thing didst thou do that the fierce flames might not consume thee; still a lasting passion settled deep in thy reluctant breast. Thou, who wast able to change men into a thousand shapes, wast not able to change the bent of thy own inclination. Thou art said to have detained the Lulicillan chief, when now he wished to depart, even in these words:

"I do not now entreat that which, as I remember, I was at first wont to hope for, that thou shouldst consent to be my husband. And still, I did seem worthy to be thy wife, since I was a Goddess, since I was the daughter of the Sun. Hasten not away, I entreat thee; a little delay, as a favour, do I ask. What less can he prayed for by my entreaties? Thou seest, too, that the seas are troubled; and of them thou oughtst to stand in dread. Before long, the winds will be more favourable to thy sails. What is the cause of thy flight? No Troy is rising here anew; no fresh Rhesus is calling his companions to arms. Here love abides, here peace exists; during which I alone am fatally wounded; the whole, too, of my realms shall be under thy sway."

She thus spoke; Ulysses unmoored his bark; the South winds bore away her unavailing words together with his sails. Circe was inflamed, and had recourse to her wonted arts; and still by them her passion was not diminished.

Come, then, whoever you are, that require aid from my skill, away with all belief in spells and charms. If some weighty reason shall detain you in the City mistress of the world, hear what is my advice in the City. He is the best assertor of his liberties who bursts the chains that gall his breast, and once for all ceases to grieve. If any one has so much courage, even I myself will admire him, and I shall say, "This man stands in no need of my admonitions." You who with difficulty are learning how not to love the object which you love; who are not able, and still would wish to be able, will require to be instructed by me. Full oft recall to your remembrance the deeds of the perfidious fair one, and place all your losses before your eyes.' Say, "This thing and that of mine does she keep; and not content with that spoliation, she has put up for sale my paternal home. Thus did she swear to me; thus having sworn, did she deceive me. How oft has she suffered me to be before her doors! She herself loves other men; by me she loathes to be loved. Some hawker, alas! enjoys those nights which she grants not to myself."

Let all these points ferment throughout your entire feelings; repeat them over and over hence seek the first germs of your hate. And would that you could be even eloquent upon them! Do' you only grieve; of your own accord you will be fluent. My attentions were lately paid to a certain fair one; to my passion she was not favourably disposed. Sick, like Podalirius, I cured myself with the proper herbs, and (I confess it) though a physician, to my shame, I was sick. It did me good to be ever dwelling upon the failings of my mistress; and that, when done, often proved wholesome for me. "How ill formed," I used to say, "are the legs of my mistress!" and yet, to confess the truth, they were not. "How far from beautiful are the arms of my mistress!" and yet, to confess the truth, they were. "How short she is!" and yet she was not; "How much does she beg of her lover?" From that arose the greatest cause of my hatred.

There are good qualities, too, near akin to bad ones; by reason of confounding one for the other, a virtue has often borne the blame for a vice. So far as you can, depreciate the endowments of the fair one, and impose upon your own judgment by the narrow line that separates good from bad. If she is embonpoint, let her be called flabby, if she is swarthy, black. Leanness may be charged against her slender form. She, too, who is not coy may be pronounced bold; and if she is discreet, she may be pronounced a prude. Besides, in whatever accomplishment your mistress is deficient, ever be entreating her, in complimentary accents, to turn her attention to the same. If any damsel is without a voice, request her to sing; if any fair one does not know how to move her hands with gracefulness, make her dance. Is she imeouth in her language, make her talk frequently to you; has she not learnt how to touch the strings, call for the lyre.

Does she walk heavily, make her walk; does a swelling bosom cover all her breast, let no stomacher conceal it. If her teeth are bad, tell her something for her to laugh at: is she tender-eyed, relate something for her to weep at.

It will be of use, too, for you, early in the morning suddenly, to turn your hasty steps towards your mistress, when she has dressed for no one. By dress are we enchanted; by gems and gold all things are concealed; the fair one herself is but a very trifling part of herself. Often, amid objects so many, you may inquire what it is that you love. By this Ægis does Love, amid his riches, deceive the eye. Come unexpectedly; in safety to yourself you will find her unarmed; to her misfortune, through her own failings will she fall. Still, it is not safe to trust too much to this precept, for without the resources of art a graceful form captivates many. At the moment, too, when she shall be smearing her face with the cosmetics laid on it, you may come in the presence of your mistress, and don't let shame prevent you. You will find there boxes, and a thousand colours of objects; and you will see cesypum, the ointment of the fleece, trickling down and flowing upon her heated bosom. These drugs, Phineus, smell like thy tables; not once only has sickness been caused by this to my stomach.

Now will I disclose to you, what should be done in the moments of your transport; from every quarter must love be put to flight. Many of them, indeed, I am ashamed to mention; but do you conceive in your imagination even more than lies in my words. For, of late, certain persons have been blaming my treatises, in the opinion of whom my Muse is wanton. If I only please, and so long as I am celebrated all the world over, let this person or that attack my work just as he likes. Envy detracts from the genius of mighty Homer; whoever thou art, from him, Zoilus, dost thou derive thy fame.

Sacrilegious hands have also mangled thy poems, thou, under whose guidance Troy brought hither her conquered Divinities. Envy takes a lofty flight; on high the breezes sweep along; the lightnings hurled by the right hand of Jove take a lofty range.

But you, whoever you are, whom my freedom offends, require, if you are wise, each subject for its proper numbers. Bold warfare delights to be related in the Mæonian measure. What place can there be there for *gentle* dalliance? The Tragedians speak in lofty tones; anger befits the buskin of Tragedy; the sock *of Comedy* must be furnished from the manners of every-day life. The free Iambic measure may be launched against the hostile foe; whether it be rapid, or whether it drag on its foot at its close. Soft Elegy should sing of the Loves with their quivers, and the sprightly mistress ought to sport according to her own inclination. Achilles is not to be celebrated in the numbers of Callimachus; Cydippe belongs not, Homer, to thy song. Who could endure Thais performing the part of Andromache? If any one were to act Thais in the tones of Andromache, he would be making a mistake. Thais belongs to my purse; licence unrestrained belongs to me. Nought have I to do with the fillet *of chastity*; Thais belongs to my pursuit. If my Muse is befitting a sportive subject, I have conquered, and on a false charge she has been accused.

Burst thyself, gnawing Envy; now have I gained great fame; 'twill be still greater, let it only proceed with the steps with which it has commenced. But you are making too great haste; let me only live, you shall have more to complain of; my intentions, too, embrace full many a poem. For it gives me delight, and my zeal increases with my eagerness for fame; at the beginning of the ascent only is my steed now panting. Elegy acknowledges that to me she is as much indebted as is the noble Epic to Virgil.

Thus far do I give an answer to Envy; tighten the reins with more vigour, and speed onward, Poet, in thy circle:

> *Ergo ubi concubitus, et opus juvenile petetur;*
> *Et prope promissæ tempora noctis erunt;*
> *Gaudia ne dominæ, pleno si pectore sùmes,*
> *Te capiant: ineas quamlibet ante velim.*
> *Quamlibet invenias, in qua tibi prima voluptas*
> *Desinat: a primâ proxima segnis erit.*
> *Sustentata Venus gratissima: frigore soles,*
> *Sole juvant umbræ: grata fit unda siti.*
> *Et pu' det, et dicam, Venerem quoque junge figurâ,*
> *Quâ minime jungi quamque decere putes.*

And 'tis no hard matter to do this; few women confess the truth to themselves; and there is no point in which they think that they are unbecoming. Then, too, I recommend you to open all the windows, and to remark in full daylight the limbs that are unsightly. But as soon as your transports have come to a termination, and the body with the mind lies entirely exhausted; while you are feeling regret, and wishing that you had formed a connexion with no female, and are seeming to yourself that for a long time you will have nothing to do with another; then note in your memory whatever blemishes there are in her person; and keep your eyes always fixed upon her faulty points.

Perhaps some one will pronounce these matters trivial (for indeed they are so); but things which, singly, are of no avail, when united are of benefit. The little viper kills with its sting the bulky bull; by the dog that is not large, full oft is the boar held fast. Do you only fight with a number of them, and unite my precepts together; from so many there will be a large amount. But since there are so many ways and attitudes, every point is not to be yielded to my recommendations. Perhaps, in the opinion of another, that will be a fault, by the doing of which your feelings may not be hurt. Because this person, perchance, has seen the charms of the naked person exposed, his passion, which was in mid career, stops short: another, when his mistress has received him, has been shocked at some sight which creates disgust.

Alas! if these things could influence you, you are trifling; torches but luke-warm have been influencing your breast. That Boy would more strongly draw his bended bow: you, ye wounded throng, will need more a substantial aid. What think you of the man who lies concealed, and beholds sights that usage itself forbids him to see? May the Gods forbid that I should advise any one to adopt such a course! Though it should prove of use, still it should not be tried.

I advise you, also, to have two mistresses at the same time. If a person can have still more, he is more secure. When the feelings, sundered into two parts, are wavering in each direction, the one passion diminishes the strength of the other. By many streamlets are great rivers lessened, and the exhausted flame, the fuel withdrawn, goes out. But one anchor does not sufficiently hold the waxed ships; a single hook is not enough for the flowing stream. He who beforehand has provided for himself a twofold solace, has already proved the victor in the lofty citadel. But, by you, who, to your misfortune, have devoted yourself to but one mistress, now, at all events, a new passion must be sought. For Procris did Minos abandon his flame for Pasiphaë; overcome by the wife from Ida, the first wife gave way. Calirrhoë, received to a share of his couch, caused the brother of Amphilochus not always to be in love with the daughter of Phegeus. Oeuone, too, would have retained Paris to her latest years, if she had not been supplanted by her Aebalian rival. The beauty of his wife would have pleased the Odrysian tyrant, but superior were the charms of her imprisoned sister.

Why occupy myself with illustrations, the number of which exhausts me? Every passion is conquered by a fresh successor. With greater fortitude does a mother regret one out of many, than she who, weeping, exclaims: "Thou wast my only one." But lest, perchance, you should suppose that I am framing new laws for you, (and would that the glory of the discovery were my own!) the son of Atreus perceived this; for what could he not see, under whose command was the whole of Greece? He, victorious, loved Chryseis, captured by his own arms; but her aged parent foolishly went crying in every direction. Why dost thou weep, troublesome old man? They are well suited for each other. By thy affection, foolish man, thou art doing an injury to thy child. After Calchas, secure under the protection of Achilles, had ordered her to be restored, and she was received back to the house of her father: "There is," said the son of Atreus, "another fair one very closely resembling her beauty; and if the first syllable would allow of it, the name would, be the same; Achilles, if he were wise, would give her up to me of his own accord; if not, he will experience my might. But if any one of you, ye Greeks, disapproves of this deed; 'tis something to wield the sceptre with a powerful hand. For if I am your king, and if she does not pass her nights with me, then let Thersites succeed to my sway." Thus he said; and he had her as his great consolation for her predecessor; and the first passion was entombed in a new passion. By the example, then, of Agamemnon, admit a fresh flame, that your love may be severed in two directions. If you inquire where you are to find them? Go and read through my treatises on the art of Love; then may your bark speed on, well freighted with the fair.

But if my precepts are of any avail, if by my lips Apollo teaches aught that is advantageous to mortals; although, to your misfortune, you should be burning in the midst of Ætna, take care to appear to your mistress more cold than ice. Pretend, too, that you are unhurt; if, perchance, you should grieve at all, let her not perceive it; and laugh when, within yourself, you could have wept. I do not bid you to sever your passion in the very midst; the laws of my sway are not so harsh as that. Pretend to be that which you are not, and feign that your ardour is renounced; so, in reality, you will become what you are practising to be. Often, that I might not drink, I have wished to appear asleep; while I have so seemed, I have surrendered my conquered eyes to slumber. I have laughed at his being deceived, who was pretending that he was in love; and the fowler has fallen into his own nets.

Through habit does love enter the mind; through habit is it forgotten. He who will, be able to pretend that he is unhurt, will be unhurt. Does she tell you to come on a night appointed, do you come. Should you come, and the gate be closed; put up with it. Neither utter blandishments, nor yet utter reproaches against the door-post, and do not lay down your sides upon the hard threshold. The next morning comes; let your words be without complaints, and bear no signs of grief upon your features. She will soon lay aside her haughtiness, when she shall see you growing cool: this advantage, too, will you be gaining from my skill. And yet do you deceive yourself as well, and let not this be the end of your love. Full oft does the horse struggle against the reins when presented. Let your object lie concealed; that will come to pass which you shall not avow. The nets that are too easily seen, the bird avoids.

Let her not congratulate herself so much that she can hold you in contempt; take courage, that to your courage she may yield. Her door is open, perchance; though she should call you back, do you go out. A night is named; doubt whether you can come on the night appointed. 'Tis an easy thing to be able to endure this; unless you are deficient in wisdom, you may more readily derive amusement from one more condescending. And can any person call my precepts harsh? Why, I am acting the part of a reconciler even. For as some dispositions vary, I am varying my precepts as well. There are a thousand forms of the malady; a thousand forms of cure will there be. Some bodies are with difficulty healed by the sharp iron: potions and herbs have proved an aid to many. You are too weak, and cannot go away, and are held in bonds, and cruel Love is treading your neck beneath his foot. Cease your struggling; let the winds bring back your sails; and whither the tide calls you, thither let your oars proceed.

That thirst, parched by which you are perishing, must be satisfied by you; I permit it; now may you drink in the midst of the stream. But drink even more than what your appetite requires; make the water you have swallowed flow back from your filled throat. Always enjoy the company of your mistress, no one preventing it; let her occupy your nights, her your days. Make satiety your object; satiety puts an end to evils even. And even now, when you think you can do without her, do you remain with her. Until you have fully cloyed yourself, and satiety removes your passion, let it not please you to move from the house you loathe. That love, too, which distrust nurtures, is of long endurance; should you wish to lay this aside, lay aside your apprehensions. Who fears that she may not be his own, and that some one may rob him of her, that person will be hardly curable with the skill of Machaon. Of two sons, a mother generally loves him the most, for whose return she feels apprehensions, because he is bearing arms.

There is, near the Collinian gate, a venerable temple; the lofty Ervx gave this temple its name. There, is Lethæan Love, who heals the mind; and in cold water does he place his torches. There, too, in their prayers, do the youths pray for forgetfulness; and any fair one, if she has been smitten by an obdurate man. He thus said to me; (I am in doubt whether it was the real Cupid, or whether a vision; but I think it was a vision.)

"O Naso, thou who dost sometimes cause, sometimes relieve, the passion full of anxiety, add this to thy precepts as well. Let each person recall to mind his own mishaps; let him dismiss love; to all has the Deity assigned more or less of woes. He that stands in awe of the Puteal and of Janus, and of the Calends swiftly coming, let the borrowed sum of money be his torment. He whose father is harsh, though other things should prove to his wish, before his eyes must his harsh father be placed. Another one is living wretchedly with a wife poorly dowried, let him think that his wife is an obstacle to his fortune. You have a vineyard, on a generous soil, fruitful in choice grapes; be in dread lest the shooting grape should be blighted. Another has à ship on its return home; let him be always thinking that the sea is boisterous, and that the sea-shore is polluted by his losses. Let a son in service be the torment of one, a marriageable daughter of yourself. And who is there that has not a thousand causes for anxiety? That, Paris, thou mightst hate thine own *cause of sorrow*, thou oughtst to have placed the deaths of thy brothers before thine eyes."

Still more was he saying, when the childish form deserted my placid slumber, if slumber only it was. What am I to do? In the midst of the waves Palinurus deserts my bark; I am forced to enter on an unknown track. Whoever you are that love, avoid solitary spots; solitary spots are injurious. Whither are you flying? In the throng you may be in greater safety. You have no need of lonely places (lonesome spots increase the frenzy); the multitude will bring you aid. You will be sad, if you are alone; and before your eyes will stand the form of your forsaken mistress, as though her own self. For this reason is the night more melancholy than the hours of sunshine; the throng of your companions is then wanting to moderate your affliction.

And fly not from conversation, nor let your door be closed; and do not, in tears, hide your countenance in the shade. Always have a Pylades to console his Orestes; this, too, will prove no slight advantage in friendship. What but the solitary woods injured Phyllis? The cause of her death is well known; she was without a companion. She was going, just as the barbarous multitude celebrating the triennial sacrifice to the Edonian Bacchus, is wont to go, with dishevelled locks. And at one time, as far as she could, she looked out upon the wide ocean; at another, in her weariness, she lay her down upon the sandy shore. "Perfidious Demophoon!" she cried aloud to the deaf waves; and her words, as she grieved, were interrupted by sobs. There was a narrow path, a little darkened by the long shadows, along which, full oft, did she turn her steps towards the sea. Her ninth journey was being paced by her in her wretchedness. "See thou to this," says she; and, turning pale, she eyes her girdle. She looks, too, on the boughs; she hesitates, and she recoils at that which she dares to do; and she shudders, and then she raises her fingers to her throat.

Sithonian damsel, I would that, then, at least, thou hadst not been alone; ye woods, your foliage lost, you would not then have lamented Phyllis. Ye men that are offended by your mistresses, ye fair that are affronted by the men, from the example of Phyllis, shun too lonesome spots. A youth had done whatever my Muse recommended him, and was almost in the haven of his safety. When he came amid the eager lovers, he relapsed, and Love resumed the weapons which he had laid aside. If any one of you is loving, and does not wish to do so; do you take care, and avoid the contagion. This is often wont to injure the herds as well. While the eyes are looking on the wounded, they themselves are also wounded; many things, too, injure the body by infection. Sometimes water flows from a river that runs near into a spot parched with its dry clods. Love flows on concealedly, if you do not withdraw from him who loves; and we are all of us a set clever at running that risk.

A second one had now been healed; his nearness to her affected him. He proved unable to endure meeting with his mistress. The scar, not sufficiently closed, changed again into the former wound; and my skill met with no success. The fire next door is guarded against with difficulty; 'tis prudent to keep away from the neighbouring haunts. Let not that Portico which is wont to receive her as she walks, receive you as well; and let not the same attentions now be paid. Of what use is it to rekindle the feelings, that have cooled, by my advice? Another region must be resorted to, if you can do so. When hungry, you will not be easily restrained, the table being laid; the gushing water, too, provokes excessive thirst. 'Tis no easy matter to hold back the bull when he sees the heifer; on seeing the mare, the high-mettled steed is always neighing after her.

When this you have done, when at last you reach the shore, 'tis not enough for you to have abandoned her. Both her sister and her mother must bid you farewell, her nurse, too, her confidant, and whatever other connexion there shall be of your mistress. And let no servant come; and let no little handmaid, feigning to weep, say to you in the name of her mistress, "Hail!" Nor yet, though you should desire to know, should you ask how she is doing. Defer it; the restraint of the tongue will be to its own advantage.

You, too, who are telling the cause of your liason being discontinued, and are relating many things to be complained of about your mistress; forbear to complain; so, by being silent, you will be taking a better revenge; until she shall vanish from your regrets. And I would rather that you were silent, than that you should talk about having cut her. The man who is too often saying to many a one, "I love her not," is still in love. But with greater certainty is the flame extinguished by degrees, than all of a sudden; cease gradually, and you will be safe. The torrent is wont to run with greater violence than the uninterrupted river; but yet the one is a short-lived, the other a lasting, stream. Let love escape you, and let it depart vanishing into thin air, and let it die out by degrees imperceptible.

But 'tis a crime to hate the fair one so lately loved; such a termination as that is befitting a brutal disposition. 'Tis enough not to care for her; he who terminates his love with hate, either still loves on, or with difficulty will cease to be wretched. 'Tis a shocking thing for a man and a woman so lately united to be enemies at once; the Appian Goddess herself would not approve of such quarrels as those. Full oft do men accuse their mistresses, and still they love them: where no discord arises, Love released, through advice, betakes himself away.

By chance I was in the company of a young man; a litter contained his mistress; all his expressions were shocking from his frightful threats; and now, about to cite her at law, he said, "Let her come out of the litter!" She did come out; on seeing his mistress, he was dumb. His hands both fell, and his two tablets from out of his hands. He rushed into her em braces; and "thus," said he, "do you prove the conqueror."

'Tis more safe, and more becoming, to depart in peace, than from the chamber to repair to the litigious Courts. The presents which you have given her, request her to keep without litigation; trivial losses are wont to be of great benefit. But if any accident should bring you together, keep those arms of defence which I am giving, firmly fixed in your mind. Then, there is need of arms; here, most valorous man, use your energies. By your weapon must Penthesilea be overcome. Now let the rival, now the obdurate threshold, when you were her lover, recur to you; now your words uttered in vain in presence of the Gods. Neither arrange your hair, because you are about to approach her; nor let your robe be seen with loose folds upon the bosom. Have no care to be pleasing to the alienated fair one; now make her to be one of the multitude so far as you are concerned.

But I will tell what especially stands in the way of my endeavours; his own example instructing each individual. We cease to love by slow degrees, because we hope to be loved ourselves; and while each one is satisfying himself, we are ever a credulous set. But do you believe that, in her oaths, neither words (for what is there more deceptive than them?) nor the immortal Deities have any weight. Take care, too, not to be moved by the tears of the fair; they have instructed their eyes how to weep. By arts innumerable are the feelings of lovers laid siege to; just as the rock that is beaten on every side by the waves of the sea. And do not disclose the reasons why you would prefer a separation, nor tell her what you take amiss; still, to yourself, ever grieve on.

And don't recount her failings, lest she should extenuate them. You yourself will prove indulgent; so that her cause will prove better than your own cause. He that is silent, is strong in his resolution; he that utters many reproaches to the fair one, asks for himself to be satisfied by her justification. I would not venture, after the example of him of Dulichium, to dip the vengeful arrows, nor the glowing torches, in the stream; I shall not clip the empurpled wings of the Boy, the God of Love; nor through my skill shall his hallowed bow be unstrung. 'Tis in accordance with prudence, whatever I sing. Give heed to me as I sing; and Phoebus, giver of health, as thou art wont, be thou propitious to my attempts.

Phoebus is propitious; his lyre sounds; his quiver resounds. By his signs do I recognize the God; Phoebus is propitious. Compare the fleece that has been dyed in the cauldrons of Amyclæ with the Tyrian purple; the former will be but dull. Do you, too, compare your charmers with the beauteous fair; each one will begin to be ashamed of his own mistress. Both Juno and Pallas may have seemed beauteous to Paris: but Venus surpassed them both when compared with herself. And not the appearance only; compare the manners and the accomplishments as well; only let not your passion prejudice your judgment.

What I shall henceforth sing is but trifling; but trifling as it is, it has proved of service to many; among whom I myself was one. Take care not to read over again the letters that you have kept of the caressing fair one: letters, when read over again, shake even a firm determination. Put the whole of them (though unwillingly you should put them) into the devouring flames; and say, "May this prove the funeral pile of my passion." The daughter of Thestius burned her son Meleager afar off by means of the billet. Will you, with hesitation, commit the words of perfidy to the flames? If you can, remove her waxen portrait as well. Why be moved by a dumb likeness? By this means was Laodamia undone. Many localities, too, have bad effects: fly from the spots that were conscious of your embraces; a thousand grounds for sorrow do they contain. Here she has been; here she has laid; in that chamber have we slept; here, in the voluptuous night, has she yielded to me her embraces.

By recollection, love is excited afresh, and the wound renewed is opened; a trifling cause is injurious to the sickly. As, if you were to touch ashes almost cold with sulphur, they would rekindle, and, from a small one, a very great fire would be produced; so, unless you avoid whatever renews love, the flame will be kindled afresh, which just now was not existing. The Argive ships would fain have fled from Caphareus, and from thee, old man, that didst avenge thy woes with the flames. The daughter of Nisus past by, the cautious mariner rejoices. Do you avoid the spots which have proved too delightful for you. Let these be your Syrtes; avoid these as your Acroceraunia; here does the ruthless Charybdis vomit forth and swallow down the waves. Some things there are which cannot be recommended at the bidding of any one; still, the same, if happening by chance, are often wont to be of service.

Had Phædra lost her wealth, thou wouldst, Neptune, have spared thy descendant; nor would the bull, sent by his ancestor, have startled the steeds. Had you made the Gnossian damsel poor, she would have loved with prudence. Voluptuous passion is nourished by opulence. Why was there no one to court Hecale, no one to court Iras? It was because the one was in want, the other a pauper. Poverty has nothing by which to pamper its passion; still, this is not of so much consequence, that you should desire to be poor.

But let it be of so much consequence to you, as not to be indulging yourself with the Theatres, until Love has entirely departed from your liberated breast. The harps, and the pipes, and the lyres, soften the feelings; the voices, too, and the arms, moved to their proper time. There, everlastingly, the parts of supposed lovers are being acted in the dance; by his skill, the actor teaches you what to avoid, and what is serviceable. Unwillingly must I say it: meddle not with the amorous Poets; unnaturally do I myself withhold my own productions. Avoid Callimachus; no enemy is he to Love; and together with Callimachus, thou, too, bard of Cos, art injurious. Beyond a doubt, Sappho has rendered me more lenient to my mistress; and the Teian Muse has imparted manners far from austere. Who can read in safety the lines of Tibullus, or thine, thou, whose sole subject Cynthia was? Who, after reading Gallus, could retire with obdurate feelings? Even my own lines have tones indescribably sweet.

Unless Apollo, the inspirer of my work, is deceiving his bard, a rival is the especial cause of our torments. But do you refrain from conjuring up to yourself any rival; and believe that she lies alone upon her couch. Orestes loved Hermione more intensely for that very reason; because she had begun to belong to another man. Why, Menelaiis, dost thou grieve? Without thy wife thou didst go to Crete; and thou couldst, at thy ease, be absent from thy spouse. Soon as Paris has carried her off, then at last thou couldst not do without thy wife; through the passion of another was thine own increased. This, too, did Achilles lament, in the case of the daughter of Brises, when taken away from him, that she was administering to the pleasures of the couch of the son of Plisthenes. And not without reason, believe me, did he lament. The son of Atreus did that, which if he had not done, he would have been disgracefully torpid. At least, I should have done so, and 1 am not any wiser than he. That was the especial reward for the ill-will he got. For, inasmuch as he swore by his sceptre, that the daughter of Brises had never been touched by him; 'tis clear that he did not think his sceptre was the Gods.

May the Deities grant that you may be able to pass the threshold of the mistress that you have forsaken; and that your feet may aid your determination. And you will be able; do you only wish to adhere to your purpose. Now it is necessary to go with boldness, now to put spur to the swift steed. Believe that in that cave are the Lotophagi, in that the Syrens; add sail to your oars. The man, too, who being your rival, you formerly took it amiss; I would have you cease to hold him in the place of an enemy. But, at least, though the hatred should still exist, salute him. When now you shall be able to embrace him, you will be cured.

That I may perform all the duties of a physician, behold! I will tell you what food to avoid, or what to adopt. The Bauman onions, or those sent you from the Libyan shores, or whether those that come from Megara, will all prove injurious. And 'tis no less proper to avoid the lustful rocket, and whatever else provokes our bodies to lust. To more advantage may you use rue that sharpens the sight, and whatever guards our bodies against lust. Do you enquire what I would advise you about the gifts of Bacchus? You will be satisfied thereon by my precepts sooner than you expect. Wine incites the feelings to lust, unless you take it in great quantities, and, drenched with much liquor, your senses become stupefied. By wind is fire kindled, by wind is it extinguished. A gentle breeze nourishes flame, a stronger one puts it out. Either let there be no drunkenness, or to so great an extent as to remove your anxieties; if there is any medium between the two, it is injurious.

This work have I completed; present the garlands to my wearied bark. I have reached the harbour, whither my course was directed. Both females and males, healed by my lays, to the Poet ere long will you be fulfilling your duteous vows.

A Note About the Author

Ovid (43 BC–17/18 AD) was a Roman poet. Born in Sulmo the year after Julius Caesar's assassination, Ovid would join the ranks of Virgil and Horace to become one of the foremost poets of Augustus' reign as first Roman emperor. After rejecting a life in law and politics, he embarked on a career as a poet, publishing his first work, the *Heroides*, in 19 BC. This was quickly followed by his *Amores* (16 BC), a collection of erotic elegies written to his lover Corinna. By 8 AD, Ovid finished his *Metamorphoses*, an epic narrative poem tracing the history of Rome and the world from the creation of the cosmos to the death and apotheosis of Julius Caesar. Ambitious and eminently inspired, *Metamorphoses* remains a timeless work of Roman literature and an essential resource for the study of classical languages and mythology. Exiled that same year by Augustus himself, Ovid spent the rest of his life in Tomis on the Black Sea, where he continued to write poems of loss, repentance and longing.

A Note from the Publisher

Spanning many genres, from non-fiction essays to literature classics to children's books and lyric poetry, Mint Edition books showcase the master works of our time in a modern new package. The text is freshly typeset, is clean and easy to read, and features a new note about the author in each volume. Many books also include exclusive new introductory material. Every book boasts a striking new cover, which makes it as appropriate for collecting as it is for gift giving. Mint Edition books are only printed when a reader orders them, so natural resources are not wasted. We're proud that our books are never manufactured in excess and exist only in the exact quantity they need to be read and enjoyed.

bookfinity™

Discover more of your favorite classics with Bookfinity™.

- Track your reading with custom book lists.
- Get great book recommendations for your personalized Reader Type.
- Add reviews for your favorite books.
- AND MUCH MORE!

Visit **bookfinity.com** and take the fun Reader Type quiz to get started.

Enjoy our classic and modern companion pairings!

Classic & Modern